W. S. GRAHAM

Selected Poems

———

ff

faber and faber

LONDON · BOSTON

First published in Great Britain in 1996
by Faber and Faber Ltd
3 Queen Square London WC1N 3AU

Phototypeset by Wilmaset Ltd, Birkenhead, Wirral
Printed in England by Clays Ltd, St Ives plc

© The Estate of W. S. Graham, 1996

A CIP record for this book
is available from the British Library

ISBN 0-571-17659-3

2 4 6 8 10 9 7 5 3 1

Please renew/return this item by the last date shown.

So that your telephone call is charged at local rate,
please call the numbers as set out below:

	From Area codes 01923 or 020:	From the rest of Herts:
Renewals:	01923 471373	01438 737373
Enquiries:	01923 471333	01438 737333
Textphone:	01923 471599	01438 737599

L32 www.hertsdirect.org/librarycatalogue

CONTENTS

LISTEN. PUT ON MORNING

Listen. Put on morning.
Waken into falling light.
A man's imagining
Suddenly may inherit
The handclapping centuries
Of his one minute on earth.
And hear the virgin juries
Talk with his own breath
To the corner boys of his street.
And hear the Black Maria
Searching the town at night.
And hear the playropes caa
The sister Mary in.
And hear Willie and Davie
Among bracken of Narnain
Sing in a mist heavy
With myrtle and listeners.
And hear the higher town
Weep a petition of fears
At the poorhouse close upon
The public heartbeat.
And hear the children tig
And run with my own feet
Into the netting drag
Of a suiciding principle.
Listen. Put on lightbreak.
Waken into miracle.
The audience lies awake
Under the tenements

Under the sugar docks
Under the printed moments.
The centuries turn their locks
And open under the hill
Their inherited books and doors
All gathered to distil
Like happy berry pickers
One voice to talk to us.
Yes listen. It carries away
The second and the years
Till the heart's in a jacket of snow
And the head's in a helmet white
And the song sleeps to be wakened
By the morning ear bright.
Listen. Put on morning.
Waken into falling light.

THE HILL OF INTRUSION

The ear the answer
Hears the wrecked cry
Of the one-time
Holiday boy who
Feathered his oars
On a calm firth
Held still by hills.
Now grey rock clenches
Round the rower over-
Taken by rough
White-haired sea-troughs
That ride the foam
Of Time's bare back.
Wrecked pile of past
Events cindered
Into a charcoal
Of kindling power
And constellations
Of united hearts,
These make reply
To the flare flying
Off from the endangered
Watchman wornout.
The winds from a hill
Halfway Ben Narnain
And halfway hill
Of intrusion into
The silence between
My heart and those

Elements of nature
That are my food,
Sound out alarm
Over the baling
Prisoners of water
This night unsheltered.
The ear says more
Than any tongue.
The ear sings better
Than any sound
It hears on earth
Or waters perfect.
The ear the answer
Hears the caged cry
Of those prisoners
Crowded in a gesture
Of homesickness.

THE CHILDREN OF GREENOCK

Local I'll bright my tale on, how
She rose up white on a Greenock day
Like the one first-of-all morning
On earth, and heard children singing.

She in a listening shape stood still
In a high tenement at Spring's sill
Over the street and chalked lawland
Peevered and lined and fancymanned

On a pavement shouting games and faces.
She saw them children of all cries
With everyone's name against them bled
In already the helpless world's bed.

Already above the early town
The smoky government was blown
To cover April. The local orient's
Donkeymen, winches and steel giants

Wound on the sugar docks. Clydeside,
Webbed in its foundries and loud blood,
Binds up the children's cries alive.
Her own red door kept its young native.

Her own window by several sights
Wept and became the shouting streets.
And her window by several sights
Adored the even louder seedbeats.

She leaned at the bright mantle brass
Fairly a mirror of surrounding sorrows,
The sown outcome of always war
Against the wordperfect, public tear.

Brighter drifted upon her the sweet sun
High already over all the children
So chained and happy in Cartsburn Street
Barefoot on authority's alphabet.

Her window watched the woven care
Hang webbed within the branched and heavy
Body. It watched the blind unborn
Copy book after book of sudden

Elements within the morning of her
Own man-locked womb. It saw the neighbour
Fear them housed in her walls of blood.
It saw two towns, but a common brood.

Her window watched the shipyards sail
Their men away. The sparrow sill
Bent grey over the struck town clocks
Striking two towns, and fed its flocks.

GIGHA

That firewood pale with salt and burning green
Outfloats its men who waved with a sound of drowning
Their saltcut hands over mazes of this rough bay.

Quietly this morning beside the subsided herds
Of water I walk. The children wade the shallows.
The sun with long legs wades into the sea.

AS BRILLIANCE FELL

As brilliance fell I girded me with voice.

But always all words waste from inward out
And I who was fastened to that furious choice
Turned out to hear myself as a contrary shout.

As the night signed I made making my house.

Yet always all words waste and alter into
A formal ruin lesser than that voice
So clenched in prison in my mortal tree.

At final night I perished into words.

And always all words ill-devise the tongue
That at poor best must sing the beast it guards.
As his blood sang the poem-imprisoned king

Sang me more than myself and made the whole
Descended house of night my house excel.

THE NIGHTFISHING

I

Very gently struck
The quay night bell.

Now within the dead
Of night and the dead
Of my life I hear
My name called from far out.
I'm come to this place
(Come to this place)
Which I'll not pass
Though one shall pass
Wearing seemingly
This look I move as.
This staring second
Breaks my home away
Through always every
Night through every whisper
From the first that once
Named me to the bone.
Yet this place finds me
And forms itself again.
This present place found me.
Owls from on the land.
Gulls cry from the water.
And that wind honing
The roof-ridge is out of
Nine hours west on the main

Ground with likely a full
Gale unwinding it.

Gently the quay bell
Strikes the held air.

Strikes the held air like
Opening a door
So that all the dead
Brought to harmony
Speak out on silence.

I bent to the lamp. I cupped
My hand to the glass chimney.
Yet it was a stranger's breath
From out of my mouth that
Shed the light. I turned out
Into the salt dark
And turned my collar up.

And now again almost
Blindfold with the bright
Hemisphere unprised
Ancient overhead,
I am befriended by
This sea which utters me.

The hull slewed out through
The lucky turn and trembled
Under way then. The twin
Screws spun sweetly alive
Spinning position away.

Far out faintly calls
The continual sea.

Now within the dead
Of night and the dead
Of all my life I go.
I'm one ahead of them
Turned in below.
I'm borne, in their eyes,
Through the staring world.

The present opens its arms.

2

To work at waking. Yet who wakes?
Dream gives awake its look. My death
Already has me clad anew.
We'll move off in this changing grace.
The moon keels and the harbour oil
Looks at the sky through seven colours.

When I fell down into this place
My father drew his whole day's pay,
My mother lay in a set-in bed,
The midwife threw my bundle away.

Here we dress up in a new grave,
The fish-boots with their herring scales
Inlaid as silver of a good week,
The jersey knitted close as nerves
Of the ground under the high bracken.
My eyes let light in on this dark.

When I fell from the hot to the cold
My father drew his whole day's pay,
My mother lay in a set-in bed,
The midwife threw my bundle away.

I, in Time's grace, the grace of change, sail surely
Moved off the land and the skilled keel sails
The darkness burning under where I go.
Landvoices and the lights ebb away
Raising the night round us. Unwinding whitely,
My changing motive pays me slowly out.
The sea sails in. The quay opens wide its arms
And waves us loose.

So I would have it, waved from home to out
After that, the continual other offer,
Intellect sung in a garment of innocence.
Here, formal and struck into a dead stillness,
The voyage sails you no more than your own.
And on its wrought epitaph fathers itself
The sea as metaphor of the sea. The boat
Rides in its fires.

And nursed now out on movement as we go,
Running white from the bow, the long keel sheathed
In departure leaving the sucked and slackening water
As mingled in memory; night rises stooped high over
Us as our boat keeps its nets and men and
Engraves its wake. Our bow heaves hung on a likely
Bearing for fish. The Mor Light flashes astern
Dead on its second.

Across our moving local of light the gulls
Go in a wailing slant. I watch, merged
In this and in a like event, as the boat
Takes the mild swell, and each event speaks through.

They speak me thoroughly to my faintest breath.
And for what sake? Each word is but a longing
Set out to break from a difficult home. Yet in
Its meaning I am.

The weather's come round. For us it's better broken.
Changed and shifted above us, the sky is broken
Now into a few light patches brightly ground
With its rough smithers and those swells lengthening
Easy on us, outride us in a slow follow
From stern to stem. The keel in its amorous furrow
Goes through each word. He drowns, who but ill
Resembled me.

In those words through which I move, leaving a cry
Formed in exact degree and set dead at
The mingling flood, I am put forward on to
Live water, clad in oil, burnt by salt
To life. Here, braced, announced on to the slow
Heaving seaboards, almost I am now too
Lulled. And my watch is blear. The early grey
Air is blowing.

It is that first pallor there, broken, running
Back on the sheared water. Now the chill wind
Comes off the shore sharp to find its old mark
Between the shoulderblades. My eyes read in
The fixed and flying signs wound in the light
Which all shall soon lie wound in as it slowly
Approaches rising to break wide up over the
Brow of the sea.

My need reads in light more specially gendered and
Ambitioned by all eyes that wide have been
Me once. The cross-tree light, yellowing now,
Swings clean across Orion. And waned and very
Gently the old signs tilt and somersault
Towards their home. The undertow, come hard round,
Now leans the tiller strongly jammed over
On my hip-bone.

It is us at last sailed into the chance
Of a good take. For there is the water gone
Lit black and wrought like iron into the look
That's right for herring. We dropped to the single motor.
The uneasy and roused gulls slid across us with
Swelled throats screeching. Our eyes sharpened what
Place we made through them. Now almost the light
To shoot the nets,

And keep a slow headway. One last check
To the gear. Our mended newtanned nets, all ropes
Loose and unkinked, tethers and springropes fast,
The tethers generous with floats to ride high,
And the big white bladder floats at hand to heave.
The bow wakes hardly a spark at the black hull.
The night and day both change their flesh about
In merging levels.

No more than merely leaning on the sea
We move. We move on this near-stillness enough
To keep the rudder live and gripped in the keel-wash.
We're well hinted herring plenty for the taking,

About as certain as all those signs falling
Through their appearance. Gulls settle lightly forward
Then scare off wailing as the sea-dusk lessens
Over our stern.

Yes, we're right set, see, see them go down, the best
Fishmarks, the gannets. They wheel high for a moment
Then heel, slip off the bearing air to plummet
Into the schooling sea. It's right for shooting,
Fish breaking the oiled water, the sea still
Holding its fires. Right, easy ahead, we'll run
Them straight out lined to the west. Now they go over,
White float and rope

And the net fed out in arm-lengths over the side.
So we shoot out the slowly diving nets
Like sowing grain. There they drag back their drifting
Weight out astern, a good half-mile of corks
And bladders. The last net's gone and we make fast
And cut the motor. The corks in a gentle wake,
Over curtains of water, tether us stopped, lapped
At far last still.

It is us no more moving, only the mere
Maintaining levels as they mingle together.
Now round the boat, drifting its drowning curtains
A grey of light begins. These words take place.
The petrel dips at the water-fats. And quietly
The stillness makes its way to its ultimate home.
The bilges slap. Gulls wail and settle.
It is us still.

At last it's all so still. We hull to the nets,
And rest back with our shoulders slacked pleasantly.
And I am illusioned out of this flood as
Separate and stopped to trace all grace arriving.
This grace, this movement bled into this place,
Locks the boat still in the grey of the seized sea.
The illuminations of innocence embrace.
What measures gently

Cross in the air to us to fix us so still
In this still brightness by knowledge of
The quick proportions of our intricacies?
What sudden perfection is this the measurement of?
And speaks us thoroughly to the bone and has
The iron sea engraved to our faintest breath,
The spray fretted and fixed at a high temper,
A script of light.

So I have been called by my name and
It was not sound. It is me named upon
The space which I continually move across
Bearing between my courage and my lack
The constant I bleed on. And, put to stillness,
Fixed in this metal and its cutting salts,
It is this instant to exact degree,
And for whose sake?

It is this instant written dead. This instant,
Bounded by its own grace and all Time's grace,
Masters me into its measurement so that
My ghostly constant is articulated.

Then suddenly like struck rock all points unfix.
The whole east breaks and leans at last to us,
Ancient overhead. Yet not a break of light
But mingles into

The whole memory of light, and will not cease
Contributing its exiled quality.
The great morning moves from its equivalent
Still where it lies struck in expressed proportion.
The streaming morning in its tensile light
Leans to us and looks over on the sea.
It's time to haul. The air stirs its faint pressures,
A slat of wind.

We are at the hauling then hoping for it
The hard slow haul of a net white with herring
Meshed hard. I haul, using the boat's cross-heave
We've started, holding fast as we rock back,
Taking slack as we go to. The day rises brighter
Over us and the gulls rise in a wailing scare
From the nearest net-floats. And the unfolding water
Mingles its dead.

Now better white I can say what's better sighted,
The white net flashing under the watched water,
The near net dragging back with the full belly
Of a good take certain, so drifted easy
Slow down on us or us hauled up upon it
Curved in a garment down to thicker fathoms.
The hauling nets come in sawing the gunwale
With herring scales.

The air bunches to a wind and roused sea-cries.
The weather moves and stoops high over us and
There the forked tern, where my look's whetted on
    distance,
Quarters its hunting sea. I haul slowly
Inboard the drowning flood as into memory,
Braced at the breathside in my net of nerves.
We haul and drift them home. The winds slowly
Turn round on us and

Gather towards us with dragging weights of water
Sleekly swelling across the humming sea
And gather heavier. We haul and hold and haul
Well the bright chirpers home, so drifted whitely
All a blinding garment out of the grey water.
And, hauling hard in the drag, the nets come in,
The headrope a sore pull and feeding its brine
Into our hacked hands.

Over the gunwale over into our deep lap
The herring come in, staring from their scales,
Fruitful as our deserts would have it out of
The deep and shifting seams of water. We haul
Against time fallen ill over the gathering
Rush of the sea together. The calms dive down.
The strident kingforked airs roar in their shell.
We haul the last

Net home and the last tether off the gathering
Run of the started sea. And then was the first
Hand at last lifted getting us swung against
Into the homing quarter, running that white grace

That sails me surely ever away from home.
And we hold into it as it moves down on
Us running white on the hull heeled to light.
Our bow heads home

Into the running blackbacks soaring us loud
High up in open arms of the towering sea.
The steep bow heaves, hung on these words, towards
What words your lonely breath blows out to meet it.
It is the skilled keel itself knowing its own
Fathoms it further moves through, with us there
Kept in its common timbers, yet each of us
Unwound upon

By a lonely behaviour of the all common ocean.
I cried headlong from my dead. The long rollers,
Quick on the crests and shirred with fine foam,
Surge down then sledge their green tons weighing dead
Down on the shuddered deck-boards. And shook off
All that white arrival upon us back to falter
Into the waking spoil and to be lost in
The mingling world.

So we were started back over that sea we
Had worked widely all fish-seasons and over
Its shifting grounds, yet now risen up into
Such humours, I felt like a farmer tricked to sea.
For it sailed sore against us. It grew up
To black banks that crossed us. It stooped, beaked.
Its brine burnt us. I was chosen and given.
It rose as risen

Treachery becomes myself, to clip me amorously
Off from all common breath. Those fires burned
Sprigs of the foam and branching tines of water.
It rose so white, soaring slowly, up
On us, then broke, down on us. It became a mull
Against our going and unfastened under us and
Curdled from the stern. It shipped us at each blow.
The brute weight

Of the living sea wrought us, yet the boat sleeked lean
Into it, upheld by the whole sea-brunt heaved,
And hung on the swivelling tops. The tiller raised
The siding tide to wrench us and took a good
Ready hand to hold it. Yet we made a seaway
And minded all the gear was fast, and took
Our spell at steering. And we went keeled over
The streaming sea.

See how, like an early self, it's loath to leave
And stares from the scuppers as it swirls away
To be clenched up. What a great width stretches
Farsighted away fighting in its white straits
On either bow, but bears up our boat on all
Its plaiting strands. This wedge driven in
To the twisting water, we rode. The bow shores
The long rollers.

The keel climbs and, with screws spinning out of their
    bite,
We drive down into the roar of the great doorways,
Each time almost to overstay, but start
Up into again the yelling gale and hailing

Shot of the spray. Yet we should have land
Soon marking us out of this thick distance and
How far we're in. Who is that poor sea-scholar,
Braced in his hero,

Lost in his book of storms there? It is myself.
So he who died is announced. This mingling element
Gives up myself. Words travel from what they once
Passed silence with. Here, in this intricate death,
He goes as fixed on silence as ever he'll be.
Leave him, nor cup a hand to shout him out
Of that, his home. Or, if you would, O surely
There is no word,

There is not any to go over that.
It is now as always this difficult air
We look towards each other through. And is there
Some singing look or word or gesture of grace
Or naked wide regard from the encountered face,
Goes ever true through the difficult air?
Each word speaks its own speaker to his death.
And we saw land

At last marked on the tenting mist and we could
Just make out the ridge running from the north
To the Black Rosses, and even mark the dark hint
Of Skeer well starboard. Now inside the bight
The sea was loosening and the screws spun steadier
Beneath us. We still shipped the blown water but
It broke white, not green weight caved in on us.
In out of all

That forming and breaking sea we came on the long
Swell close at last inshore with the day grey
With mewing distances and mist. The rocks rose
Waving their lazy friendly weed. We came in
Moving now by the world's side. And O the land lay
Just as we knew it well all along that shore
Akin to us with each of its dear seamarks. And lay
Like a mother.

We came in, riding steady in the bay water,
A sailing pillar of gulls, past the cockle strand.
And springing teal came out off the long sand. We
Moved under the soaring land sheathed in fair water
In that time's morning grace. I uttered that place
And left each word I was. The quay-heads lift up
To pass us in. These sea-worked measures end now.
And this element

Ends as we move off from its formal instant.
Now he who takes my place continually anew
Speaks me thoroughly perished into another.
And the quay opened its arms. I heard the sea
Close on him gently swinging on oiled hinges.
Moored here, we cut the motor quiet. He that
I'm not lies down. Men shout. Words break. I am
My fruitful share.

4

Only leaned at rest
Where my home is cast
Cannonwise on silence
And the serving distance.

O my love, keep the day
Leaned at rest, leaned at rest.

Only breathed at ease
In that loneliness
Bragged into a voyage
On the maintaining image.

O my love, there we lay
Loved alone, loved alone.

Only graced in my
Changing madman who
Sings but has no time
To divine my room.

O my love, keep the day
Leaned at rest, leaned at rest.

What one place remains
Home as darkness quickens?

5

So this is the place. This
Is the place fastened still with movement,
Movement as calligraphic and formal as
A music burned on copper.

At this place
The eye reads forward as the memory reads back.
At this last word all words change.
All words change in acknowledgement of the last.
Here is their mingling element.
This is myself (who but ill resembles me).
He befriended so many
Disguises to wander in on as many roads
As cross on a ball of wool.
What a stranger he's brought to pass
Who sits here in his place.
What a man arrived breathless
With a look or word to a few
Before he's off again.

Here is this place no more
Certain though the steep streets
And High Street form again and the sea
Swing shut on hinges and the doors all open wide.

6

As leaned at rest in lamplight with
The offered moth and heard breath
By grace of change serving my birth,

And as at hushed called by the owl,
With my chair up to my salt-scrubbed table,
While my endured walls kept me still,

I leaned and with a kind word gently
Struck the held air like a doorway
Bled open to meet another's eye.

Lie down, my recent madman, hardly
Drawn into breath than shed to memory,
For there you'll labour less lonely.

Lie down and serve. Your death is past.
There the fishing ground is richest.
There contribute your sleight of cast.

The rigged ship in its walls of glass
Still further forms its perfect seas
Locked in its past transparences.

You're come among somewhere the early
Children at play who govern my way
And shed each tear which burns my eye.

Thus, shed into the industrious grave
Ever of my life, you serve the love
Whose motive we are energies of.

So quietly my words upon the air
Awoke their harmonies for ever
Contending within the ear they alter.

And as the lamp burned back the silence
And the walls caved to a clear lens,
The room again became my distance.

I sat rested at the grave's table
Saying his epitaph who shall
Be after me to shout farewell.

7

Far out, faintly rocked,
Struck the sea bell.

Home becomes this place,
A bitter night, ill
To labour at dead of.
Within all the dead of
All my life I hear
My name spoken out
On the break of the surf.
I, in Time's grace,
The grace of change, am
Cast into memory.
What a restless grace
To trace stillness on.

Now this place about me
Wakes the night's twin shafts
And sheds the quay slowly.
Very gently the keel
Walks its waters again.
The sea awakes its fires.
White water stares in
From the harbour-mouth.
And we run through well
Held off the black land
Out into the waving
Nerves of the open sea.

My dead in the crew
Have mixed all qualities
That I have been and,
Though ghosted behind

My sides spurred by the spray,
Endure by a further gaze
Pearled behind my eyes.
Far out faintly calls
The mingling sea.

Now again blindfold
With the hemisphere
Unprised and bright
Ancient overhead,

This present place is
Become made into
A breathless still place
Unrolled on a scroll
And turned to face this light.

So I spoke and died.
So within the dead
Of night and the dead
Of all my life those
Words died and awoke.

from SEVEN LETTERS

LETTER I

Welcome then anytime. Fare
Well as your skill's worth,
You able-handed sea-blade
Aglint with the inlaid
Scales of the herring host
And hosting light. Good morning
Said that. And that morning
Opened and fairly rose
Keeping sea-pace with us
Sailed out on the long kyle.
Early there I could tell
Under the scaling light
The nerves of each sheared knot
Keelcleft twisting back
Astern to make the wake,
And I saw my death flash
For an instant white like a fish
In the second-sighted sea.

That death is where I lie
In this sea you inherit.
There is no counter to it.

Taken my dear as heir
To yes again the ever
Arriving sea, I wave
Us here out on the move.
May we both fare well through
This difficult element we

Hear welcome in. Farewell
Gives us ever away
To a better host. See, I
Hack steps on the water never
For one lull still but over
Flowing all ways I make
My ways. Always I make
My ways. And as you listen
Here at the felling bow
I'll be myself in vain
Always. Dear you who walk

Your solitude on these
Words, walk their silences
Hearing a morning say
A welcome I have not heard
In words I have not made.

And the good morning rose
Fairly over the bows
And whitely waving fray.
We hauled the nets. And all
That live and silver causeway
Heaving came to our side.

These words said welcome. Fare
Them well from what they are.

LETTER II

Burned in this element
To the bare bone, I am
Trusted on the language.
I am to walk to you

[29]

Through the night and through
Each word you make between
Each word I burn bright in
On this wide reach. And you,
Within what arms you lie,
Hear my burning ways
Across these darknesses
That move and merge like foam.
Lie in the world's room,
My dear, and contribute
Here where all dialogues write.

Younger in the towered
Tenement of night he heard
The shipyards with nightshifts
Of lathes turning their shafts.
His voice was a humble ear
Hardly turned to her.
Then in a welding flash
He found his poetry arm
And turned the coat of his trade.
From where I am I hear
Clearly his heart beat over
Clydeside's far hammers
And the nightshipping firth.
What's he to me? Only
Myself I died from into
These present words that move.
In that high tenement
I got a great grave.

Tonight in sadly need
Of you I move inhuman
Across this space of dread

And silence in my mind.
I walk the dead water
Burning language towards
You where you lie in the dark
Ascension of all words.
Yet where? Where do you lie
Lost to my cry and hidden
Away from the world's downfall?
O offer some way tonight
To make your love take place
In every word. Reply.
Time's branches burn to hear.
Take heed. Reply. Here
I am driven burning on
This loneliest element. Break
Break me out of this night,
This silence where you are not,
Nor any within earshot.
Break break me from this high
Helmet of idiocy.

    Water water wallflower
    Growing up so high
    We are all children
    We all must die.
    Except Willie Graham
    The fairest of them all.
    He can dance and he can sing
    And he can turn his face to the wall.
    Fie, fie, fie for shame
    Turn your face to the wall again.

Yes laugh then cloudily laugh
Though he sat there as deaf

And worn to a stop
As the word had given him up.
Stay still. That was the sounding
Sea he moved on burning
His still unending cry.
That night hammered and waved
Its starry shipyard arms,
And it came to inherit
His death where these words merge.
This is his night writ large.
In Greenock the bright breath
Of night's array shone forth
On the nightshifting town.
Thus younger burning in
The best of his puny gear
He early set out
To write him to his death
And to that great breath
Taking of the sea,
The graith of Poetry.
My musing love lie down
Within his arms. He dies
Word by each word into

Myself now at this last
Word I die in. This last.

LETTER IV

Night winked and endeared
Itself to language. Huge
Over the dark verge sauntered
Half the moon. Then all

Its shoal attending stared
Down on the calm and mewing
Firth and in a bright
Breath that night became
You in these words fondly
Through me. Even becomes
Us now. And casts me always
Through who I thought I was.
May Love not cast us out.

Know me by the voice
That speaks outside my choice
And speaks our double breath
Into this formal death.

My dear, here and happy
We are cast off away
Swanning through the slow
Shallows and shearing into
The first heave of the deep
Sea's lusty founds.
And out. Lie here happy
Here on this bed of nets.
Loosen the blouse of night.
It seems no time since we
Lay down to let Love pass.
Past? For almost I stoop
Backward to pick Love up,
From where? My dear, all
You've had of me is always
Here. Lean here. Listen.
Though it is always going.
Nor does it say even
A part, but something else.

Time lowers it into bookmould
Filled with words that lied
To where they came from and
To where they went. Yet, lean
On your elbow here. Listen.

What a great way. So bright.
O the sea is meadowsweet.
That voice talking? It's from
Some family famous for
The sea. There's drink in it.
Where did he drown from, taken
By the sea's barbaric hooks?
Yet lie here, love. Listen
To that voice on the swell
(Old rogue with a skilful keel).
It is that voice which hears
The dog whelk's whimper
And the cockle's call come up
From the deep beds under
Those breaking prisms of water.
And hears old Mooney call Time
Bogtongued like doomsday over
The bar and hears Mooney's
Hanging lamp lapping
The sweet oil from its bowl.

And each word, 'this' and 'this'
Is that night and your breath
Dying on mine moved out
On always the sea moving
Neither its help nor comfort
Between us. Be held a while.

Old Calum's there. Listen.
This is his song he says,
To pass the time at the tiller.
He's sad drunk. Let him be.
He'll not see, that poor
Harper, bat-blind, stone-daft
(That cough was aconite).
Let him go on. His harp's
Some strung breastbone but sweet.
It's often enough their habit,
The old and answered not.

    Then what a fine upstander
    I was for the cause of Love.
    And what a fine woman's
    Man I went sauntering as.

    I could sing a tear out of
    The drunk or sober or deaf.
    My love would lie pleasanter
    Than ever she lay before.

    Now she who younger lay
    Lies lost in the husk of night.
    My far my vanished dears
    All in your bowers.

Fondly from a beyond
His song moved to my hand
And moves as you move now.
Yet here's the long heave
To move us through. Say
After me here. 'Unto
My person to be peer.'
And all holds us in the hull

That slides between the waving
Gates and the bow drives
Headlong through the salt
Thicket of the maiden sea.

And shall for Christsake always
Bleed down that streaming door.

LETTER VI

A day the wind was hardly
Shaking the youngest frond
Of April I went on
The high moor we know.
I put my childhood out
Into a cocked hat
And you moving the myrtle
Walked slowly over.
A sweet clearness became.
The Clyde sleeved in its firth
Reached and dazzled me.
I moved and caught the sweet
Courtesy of your mouth.
My breath to your breath.
And as you lay fondly
In the crushed smell of the moor
The courageous and just sun
Opened its door.
And there we lay halfway
Your body and my body
On the high moor. Without
A word then we went
Our ways. I heard the moor

Curling its cries far
Across the still loch.

The great verbs of the sea
Come down on us in a roar.
What shall I answer for?

LETTER VII

Blind tide emblazoning
My death forever on
The sheldrake dark, unperish
Me here this night. Unperish
Me burning in these words
Murmured and roared through
The listening brain of silence
To where she listening lies.

Are you awake listening?
Or are you sound? The tide
Slowly turns and slowly
The nets of night swing
Round to face the west.
We drift at the nets under
Continual cries wheeling.
What winging shapes of silence
Are for us? The herring
Have had their run for the night.
Our money is in the net
Or out. And now we'll haul
And run for home. Are you
Awake or sound and deep
In the bolster-buried ear
Adrift? Slip by sleep's gates.

Slip by sleep's gates and out
From your lost shire and over
The shore's long curlewing.
Move through the shallows out.
Never the like of bright
Steerers overhead
Started as now. Wended,
So many lie within
Your musing ear. Orion
Is brightly barbed. Again
The glint inlays the gunwale.
The wind is rising. I would
From the fires of this sea
Waylay the headlong dead.
Come nearer to hear. See,
There they arm themselves
With Love and wave the fray
Nearer us as they rise
Through every word. Through you
This branching sea burns
Me away. What blinded tons
Of water the world contains.
And yet now out of all
Its bellowing deeps and shoals
Let me be fond. Love,
Let me be fond awhile.

Bear these words in mind
As they bear me soundly
Beyond my reach. Through you
They love. But they in time
Do murder in that name.

Yet quick forget. It's all
Only a tale. Slowly
The great dialogues darken
Upon me and all voices
Between us move towards
Their end in this. Silence
Shapes before I draw breath.
Stay still. Listen so still.
There! Did you hear? Some ear
Speaks me by stealth to death.
Call through that time where once
You fondly strayed and a'
The flooer o' Galloway
Wad doon an dee. So soon
She fell under a thorn
And me. So it arose
A lapwing wandered us.
The song is shed and now
I'm minded of Calum, a man
Out of Kintyre or out
Of my tongue spoken and straight
The thirst chimes me back,
And words are a thirsty lot.
I have a hake in my throat.
You'll barely know his voice
Now for his millstoned life
Speaks through the branks of grief.
The unkind iron casts
His meaning out. The mute
Harp hangs with aconite.
Yet not mistake. Let him
Begin in time. Calum,
Come out from that black drouth.

We'll man the bottled barque
In Mooney's. Remember there
You first rendered the sash
Of foam your father wore.
May she be musing there
Tonight. For her I have
The length and breadth of Love
That it shall lusty keep
Her mind and body good.
Her bent is mine. Calum,
My tongue is Opening Time
And my ear is in its prime.
Ahoy Mooney. Draw back
The ancient bacchus bolts.
Stand clear of the gates.
And clear we are. So now
Calum, what will you have?
I'll call the rounds. Remember,
When we fished out of Kinmore
They made their own at the farm.
We drank it dripping hot
Out of an antique worm.
Now, Calum, here's to the keel.
Lift up your drinking arm.
I've waited so long for this,
To meet you in the eye
And in the ear. And now
All time's within our reach.
Drink and these words unperish
Us under the golden drench.

Welcome my dear as heir
To yes again the long

Song of the thorough keel
Moving us through the pitch
Of night in a half gale.
Here at the gunwale farewell
Gives us away this homeward
Night keeled into the final
Breathless element.
Always surely your bent
Is mine. Always surely
My thoroughfare is you.
And that is you by both
The high helmet of light
And by the beast rearing
To sire in the dark kiln.
Watch as you go. Hold
The mizzen there as the sea's
Branches burn and emblazon
Our death under every eye
And burn us into the brain
Of silence in these words.

The lit cardinals swing
Round as we swither off
Our course in a following sea.
Yet the bow climbs back
Shearing the amorous foam
And flourishes in this word
The angel-handed sword.

My love, soon to be held
Still in the last word,
Under out of the spray
Is best. But first, see!
By whose ambition shined

Do the signs arm themselves
So bright tonight to stride
At large for Love? Now where
You once lay lie. We all
Must die and we must all
Lie down in the beast cause.

Language becomes us. The ram
At large moves through this huge
Utterance in which we lie
Homelessly face to face.
Farewell then as your skill's
Worth, you wandering keel.
Make your best wake. Drive
Headlong through the salt
Thicket and thoroughfare
That offers her forever.

My love my love anywhere
Drifted away, listen.
From the dark rush under
Us comes our end. Endure
Each word as it breaks at last
To become our home here.
Who hears us now? Suddenly
In a stark flash the nerves
Of language broke. The sea
Cried out loud under the keel.
Listen. Now as I fall.

Listen. And silence even
Has turned away. Listen.

MALCOLM MOONEY'S LAND

I

Today, Tuesday, I decided to move on
Although the wind was veering. Better to move
Than have them at my heels, poor friends
I buried earlier under the printed snow.
From wherever it is I urge these words
To find their subtle vents, the northern dazzle
Of silence cranes to watch. Footprint on foot
Print, word on word and each on a fool's errand.
Malcolm Mooney's Land. Elizabeth
Was in my thoughts all morning and the boy.
Wherever I speak from or in what particular
Voice, this is always a record of me in you.
I can record at least out there to the west
The grinding bergs and, listen, further off
Where we are going, the glacier calves
Making its sudden momentary thunder.
This is as good a night, a place as any.

2

From the rimed bag of sleep, Wednesday,
My words crackle in the early air.
Thistles of ice about my chin,
My dreams, my breath a ruff of crystals.
The new ice falls from canvas walls.
O benign creature with the small ear-hole,
Submerger under silence, lead
Me where the unblubbered monster goes

Listening and makes his play.
Make my impediment mean no ill
And be itself a way.

A fox was here last night (Maybe Nansen's,
Reading my instruments.) the prints
All round the tent and not a sound.
Not that I'd have him call my name.
Anyhow how should he know? Enough
Voices are with me here and more
The further I go. Yesterday
I heard the telephone ringing deep
Down in a blue crevasse.
I did not answer it and could
Hardly bear to pass.

Landlice, always my good bedfellows,
Ride with me in my sweaty seams.
Come bonny friendly beasts, brother
To the grammarsow and the word-louse,
Bite me your presence, keep me awake
In the cold with work to do, to remember
To put down something to take back.
I have reached the edge of earshot here
And by the laws of distance
My words go through the smoking air
Changing their tune on silence.

3

My friend who loves owls
Has been with me all day
Walking at my ear
And speaking of old summers

When to speak was easy.
His eyes are almost gone
Which made him hear well.
Under our feet the great
Glacier drove its keel.
What is to read there
Scored out in the dark?

Later the north-west distance
Thickened towards us.
The blizzard grew and proved
Too filled with other voices
High and desperate
For me to hear him more.
I turned to see him go
Becoming shapeless into
The shrill swerving snow.

4

Today, Friday, holds the white
Paper up too close to see
Me here in a white-out in this tent of a place
And why is it there has to be
Some place to find, however momentarily
To speak from, some distance to listen to?

Out at the far-off edge I hear
Colliding voices, drifted, yes
To find me through the slowly opening leads.
Tomorrow I'll try the rafted ice.
Have I not been trying to use the obstacle
Of language well? It freezes round us all.

Why did you choose this place
For us to meet? Sit
With me between this word
And this, my furry queen.
Yet not mistake this
For the real thing. Here
In Malcolm Mooney's Land
I have heard many
Approachers in the distance
Shouting. Early hunters
Skittering across the ice
Full of enthusiasm
And making fly and,
Within the ear, the yelling
Spear steepening to
The real prey, the right
Prey of the moment.
The honking choir in fear
Leave the tilting floe
And enter the sliding water.
Above the bergs the foolish
Voices are lighting lamps
And all their sounds make
This diary of a place
Writing us both in.

Come and sit. Or is
It right to stay here
While, outside the tent
The bearded blinded go
Calming their children
Into the ovens of frost?

And what's the news? What
Brought you here through
The spring leads opening?

Elizabeth, you and the boy
Have been with me often
Especially on those last
Stages. Tell him a story.
Tell him I came across
An old sulphur bear
Sawing his log of sleep
Loud beneath the snow.
He puffed the powdered light
Up on to this page
And here his reek fell
In splinters among
These words. He snored well.
Elizabeth, my furry
Pelted queen of Malcolm
Mooney's Land, I made
You here beside me
For a moment out
Of the correct fatigue.

I have made myself alone now.
Outside the tent endless
Drifting hummock crests.
Words drifting on words.
The real unabstract snow.

THE BEAST IN THE SPACE

Shut up. Shut up. There's nobody here.
If you think you hear somebody knocking
On the other side of the words, pay
No attention. It will be only
The great creature that thumps its tail
On silence on the other side.
If you do not even hear that
I'll give the beast a quick skelp
And through Art you'll hear it yelp.

The beast that lives on silence takes
Its bite out of either side.
It pads and sniffs between us. Now
It comes and laps my meaning up.
Call it over. Call it across
This curious necessary space.
Get off, you terrible inhabiter
Of silence. I'll not have it. Get
Away to whoever it is will have you.

He's gone and if he's gone to you
That's fair enough. For on this side
Of the words it's late. The heavy moth
Bangs on the pane. The whole house
Is sleeping and I remember
I am not here, only the space
I sent the terrible beast across.
Watch. He bites. Listen gently

To any song he snorts or growls
And give him food. He means neither
Well or ill towards you. Above
All, shut up. Give him your love.

THE CONSTRUCTED SPACE

Meanwhile surely there must be something to say,
Maybe not suitable but at least happy
In a sense here between us two whoever
We are. Anyhow here we are and never
Before have we two faced each other who face
Each other now across this abstract scene
Stretching between us. This is a public place
Achieved against subjective odds and then
Mainly an obstacle to what I mean.

It is like that, remember. It is like that
Very often at the beginning till we are met
By some intention risen up out of nothing.
And even then we know what we are saying
Only when it is said and fixed and dead.
Or maybe, surely, of course we never know
What we have said, what lonely meanings are read
Into the space we make. And yet I say
This silence here for in it I might hear you.

I say this silence or, better, construct this space
So that somehow something may move across
The caught habits of language to you and me.
From where we are it is not us we see
And times are hastening yet, disguise is mortal.
The times continually disclose our home.
Here in the present tense disguise is mortal.
The trying times are hastening. Yet here I am
More truly now this abstract act become.

THE THERMAL STAIR

for the painter Peter Lanyon killed in a gliding accident 1964

I called today, Peter, and you were away.
I look out over Botallack and over Ding
Dong and Levant and over the jasper sea.

Find me a thermal to speak and soar to you from
Over Lanyon Quoit and the circling stones standing
High on the moor over Gurnard's Head where some

Time three foxglove summers ago, you came.
The days are shortening over Little Parc Owles.
The poet or painter steers his life to maim

Himself somehow for the job. His job is Love
Imagined into words or paint to make
An object that will stand and will not move.

Peter, I called and you were away, speaking
Only through what you made and at your best.
Look, there above Botallack, the buzzard riding

The salt updraught slides off the broken air
And out of sight to quarter a new place.
The Celtic sea, the Methodist sea is there.

    You said once in the Engine
    House below Morvah
    That words make their world
    In the same way as the painter's
    Mark surprises him
    Into seeing new.
    Sit here on the sparstone

In this ruin where
Once the early beam
Engine pounded and broke
The air with industry.

Now the chuck of daws
And the listening sea.

'Shall we go down' you said
'Before the light goes
And stand under the old
Tinworkings around
Morvah and St Just?'
You said 'Here is the sea
Made by alfred wallis
Or any poet or painter's
Eye it encountered.
Or is it better made
By all those vesselled men
Sometime it maintained?
We all make it again.'

Give me your hand, Peter,
To steady me on the word.

Seventy-two by sixty,
Italy hangs on the wall.
A woman stands with a drink
In some polite place
And looks at SARACINESCO
And turns to mention space.
That one if she could
Would ride Artistically
The thermals you once rode.

Peter, the phallic boys
Begin to wink their lights.
Godrevy and the Wolf
Are calling Opening Time.
We'll take the quickest way
The tin singers made.
Climb here where the hand
Will not grasp on air.
And that dark-suited man
Has set the dominoes out
On the Queen's table.
Peter, we'll sit and drink
And go in the sea's roar
To Labrador with wallis
Or rise on Lanyon's stair.

Uneasy, lovable man, give me your painting
Hand to steady me taking the word-road home.
Lanyon, why is it you're earlier away?
Remember me wherever you listen from.
Lanyon, dingdong dingdong from carn to carn.
It seems tonight all Closing bells are tolling
Across the Duchy shire wherever I turn.

I LEAVE THIS AT YOUR EAR

for Nessie Dunsmuir

I leave this at your ear for when you wake,
A creature in its abstract cage asleep.
Your dreams blindfold you by the light they make.

The owl called from the naked-woman tree
As I came down by the Kyle farm to hear
Your house silent by the speaking sea.

I have come late but I have come before
Later with slaked steps from stone to stone
To hope to find you listening for the door.

I stand in the ticking room. My dear, I take
A moth kiss from your breath. The shore gulls cry.
I leave this at your ear for when you wake.

THE DARK DIALOGUES

I

I always meant to only
Language swings away
Further before me.

Language swings away
Before me as I go
With again the night rising
Up to accompany me
And that other fond
Metaphor, the sea.
Images of night
And the sea changing
Should know me well enough.

Wanton with riding lights
And staring eyes, Europa
And her high meadow bull
Fall slowly their way
Behind the blindfold and
Across this more or less
Uncommon place.

And who are you and by
What right do I waylay
You where you go there
Happy enough striking
Your hobnail in the dark?
Believe me I would ask
Forgiveness but who
Would I ask forgiveness from?

[55]

I speak across the vast
Dialogues in which we go
To clench my words against
Time or the lack of time
Hoping that for a moment
They will become for me
A place I can think in
And think anything in,
An aside from the monstrous.

And this is no other
Place than where I am,
Here turning between
This word and the next.
Yet somewhere the stones
Are wagging in the dark
And you, whoever you are,
That I am other to,
Stand still by the glint
Of the dyke's sparstone,
Because always language
Is where the people are.

2

Almost I, yes, I hear
Huge in the small hours
A man's step on the stair
Climbing the pipeclayed flights
And then stop still
Under the stairhead gas
At the lonely tenement top.
The broken mantle roars
Or dims to a green murmur.

[56]

One door faces another.
Here, this is the door
With the loud grain and the name
Unreadable in brass.
Knock, but a small knock,
The children are asleep.
I sit here at the fire
And the children are there
And in this poem I am,
Whoever elsewhere I am,
Their mother through his mother.
I sit with the gas turned
Down and time knocking
Somewhere through the wall.
Wheesht, children, and sleep
As I break the raker up,
It is only the stranger
Hissing in the grate.
Only to speak and say
Something, little enough,
Not out of want
Nor out of love, to say
Something and to hear
That someone has heard me.
This is the house I married
Into, a room and kitchen
In a grey tenement,
The top flat of the land,
And I hear them breathe and turn
Over in their sleep
As I sit here becoming
Hardly who I know.
I have seen them hide

And seek and cry come out
Come out whoever you are
You're not het I called
And called across the wide
Wapenschaw of water.
But the place moved away
Beyond the reach of any
Word. Only the dark
Dialogues drew their breath.
Ah how bright the mantel
Brass shines over me.
Black-lead at my elbow,
Pipe-clay at my feet.
Wheesht and go to sleep
And grow up but not
To say mother mother
Where are the great games
I grew up quick to play.

3

Now in the third voice
I am their father through
Nothing more than where
I am made by this word
And this word to occur.
Here I am makeshift made
By artifice to fall
Upon a makeshift time.
But I can't see. I can't
See in the bad light
Moving (Is it moving?)
Between your eye and mine.

Who are you and yet
It doesn't matter only
I thought I heard somewhere
Someone else walking.
Where are the others? Why,
If there is any other,
Have they gone so far ahead?
Here where I am held
With the old rainy oak
And Cartsburn and the Otter's
Burn aroar in the dark
I try to pay for my keep.
I speak as well as I can
Trying to teach my ears
To learn to use their eyes
Even only maybe
In the end to observe
The behaviour of silence.
Who is it and why
Do you walk here so late
And how should you know to take
The left or the right fork
Or the way where, as a boy
I used to lie crouched
Deep under the flailing
Boughs of the roaring wood?
Or I lay still
Listening while a branch
Squeaked in the resinous dark
And swaying silences.

Otherwise I go
Only as a shell
Of my former self.
I go with my foot feeling
To find the side of the road,
My head inclined, my ears
Feathered to every wind
Blown between the dykes.
The mist is coming home.
I hear the blind horn
Mourning from the firth.
The big wind blows
Over the shore of my child
Hood in the off-season.
The small wind remurmurs
The fathering tenement
And a boy I knew running
The hide and seeking streets.
Or do these winds
In their forces blow
Between the words only?

I am the shell held
To Time's ear and you
May hear the lonely leagues
Of the kittiwake and the fulmar.

4

Or I am always only
Thinking is this the time
To look elsewhere to turn
Towards what was it
I put myself out

Away from home to meet?
Was it this only? Surely
It is more than these words
See on my side
I went halfway to meet.

And there are other times.
But the times are always
Other and now what I meant
To say or hear or be
Lies hidden where exile
Too easily beckons.
What if the terrible times
Moving away find
Me in the end only
Staying where I am always
Unheard by a fault.

So to begin to return
At last neither early
Nor late and go my way
Somehow home across
This gesture become
Inhabited out of hand.
I stop and listen over
My shoulder and listen back
On language for that step
That seems to fall after
My own step in the dark.

Always must be the lost
Or where we turn, and all
For a sight of the dark again.
The farthest away, the least
To answer back come nearest.

And this place is taking
Its time from us though these
Two people or voices
Are not us nor has
The time they seem to move in
To do with what we think
Our own times are. Even
Where they are is only
This one inhuman place.
Yet somewhere a stone
Speaks and maybe a leaf
In the dark turns over.
And whoever I meant
To think I had met
Turns away further
Before me blinded by
This word and this word.

See how presently
The bull and the girl turn
From what they seemed to say,
And turn there above me
With that star-plotted head
Snorting on silence.
The legend turns. And on
Her starry face descried
Faintly astonishment.
The formal meadow fades

Over the ever-widening
Firth and in their time
That not unnatural pair
Turn slowly home.

This is no other place
Than where I am, between
This word and the next.
Maybe I should expect
To find myself only
Saying that again
Here now at the end.
Yet over the great
Gantries and cantilevers
Of love, a sky, real and
Particular is slowly
Startled into light.

THE GREENOCK DIALOGUES

I

O Greenock, Greenock, I never will
Get back to you. But here I am,
The boy made good into a ghost
Which I will send along your streets
Tonight as the busy nightshifts
Hammer and spark their welding lights.

I pull this skiff I made myself
Across the almost midnight firth
Between Greenock and Kilkreggan.
My blades as they feather discard
The bright drops and the poor word
Which will always drown unheard.

Ah the little whirlpools go
Curling away for a moment back
Into my wake. Brigit. Cousin
Brigit Mooney, are you still there
On the Old Custom House shore?
You need not answer that, my dear.

And she is there with all the wisps
And murmurs in their far disguise.
Brigit, help with the boat up
Up over the shingle to the high
Tide mark. You've hardly changed, only
A little through the word's eye.

Take my hand this new night
And we'll go up to Cartsburn Street.
My poor father frightened to go
Down the manhole might be in.
Burns' Mary sleeps fine in
Inverkip Street far from Afton.

And here's the close, Brigit. My mother
Did those stairs a thousand times.
The top-flat door, my father's name
Scrived by his own hand in brass.
We stand here scrived on the silence
Under the hissing stairhead gas.

2

I (Who shall I be?) call across
The shore-side where like iron filings
The beasts of the tide are taken through
Their slow whirls between the words.
Where are you now, dear half-cousin
Brigit with your sandprints filling
In the Western, oystercatching morning?

This is a real place as far
As I am concerned. Come down over
The high-tide bladder-wrack and step
Over the gunwale of our good skiff.
I lean back on the bright blades
To move us out on language over
The loch in the morning, iodine air.

Abstract beasts in a morning mirror
By memory teased very far
Out of their origins. Where where
Shall I take us as the little whirl
Pools leave the blade and die back?
The house is shrinking. Yeats' hazel
Wood writes in a dwindling style.

From where I pull and feather I see
You dearly pulled towards me yet
Not moving nearer as we both
Move out over the burnished loch.
Move with the boat and keep us trim.
If it is a love we have, then it
Is only making it now, Brigit.

3

I am not trying to hide
Anything anything anything.
My half-cousin Brigit
With me rowed over the loch
And we pulled the skiff up
Up over the bladder
Wrack of the high tide
And climbed the Soor Duik ladder.

Ben Narnain is as good
A shape as any Ben
And I liked Ben Narnain
And half-cousin Brigit.
Remember she was only half

A cousin and not het.
These words play us both
About that time yet.

All this is far too
Innocently said.
I write this down to get her
Somewhere between the words.
You yourself can contribute
Somewhere between the words
If it does you any good.
I know what I climb towards.

Is that not (Will you say?)
Is that not right, Brigit?
With your naked feet printing
The oystercatching sand?
Shall I come back to Scotland,
My ear seeking the sound
Of what your words on the long
Loch have put in my mind.

After the bracken the open
Bare scree and the water
Ouzel and looking down
At the long loch. It was
I suppose fine but nothing
Now as the wind blows
Across the edge of Narnain
And the Soor Duik burn flows.

4

There are various ways to try to speak
And this is one. Cousin Brigit,
Sit steady. Keep us trim
And I will pull us out over
The early morning firth between
Kilkreggan and Greenock. I'll put my blades
Easily with all my sleight into
My home waters not to distort
The surface from its natural sound.

Behind your head, where I can see,
The sleeping warrior lies along
The Arran hills. Steady, Brigit,
If you would ride the clinkered skiff
And see the little whirlpools scooped
Into their quick life and go
Sailing away astern. O help
To keep me headed into the fair
And loud forest of high derricks
And welding lights blue in the sun.

Whoever you are you are; keep
Us trimmed and easy as we go
Gliding at each stroke through
The oily shipbuilding approaches.
We are here to listen. We are here
To hear the town in the disguise
My memory puts on it. Brigit
Is with me. Her I know. I put
Her in between the lines to love
And be alive in particulars.

Brigit, dear broken-song-tongued bag,
I'll not be jilted again. I see
You younger now this morning, urged
Towards me as I put my back
Into the oars and as I lean
Towards you feathering the dripping blades,
I think almost you are more mine
Than his who was before. Remember
Your name is Brigit Mooney, kin
To Malcolm in his slowly moving
Ultramarine cell of ice.

Brigit, take me with you and who
Ever it is who reads himself into
Our presence here in this doubtful
Curious gesture. Come, step over
The gunwale. I think, it seems we're here
On the dirty pebbles of my home
Town Greenock where somewhere Burns' Mary
Sleeps and John Galt's ghosts go
Still in the annals of their parish.

HILTON ABSTRACT

Roger, whether the tree is made
To speak or stand as a tree should
Lifting its branches over lovers
And moving as the wind moves,
It is the longed-for, loved event,
To be by another aloneness loved.

Hell with this and hell with that
And hell with all the scunnering lot.
This can go and that can go
And leave us with the quick and slow.
And quick and slow are nothing much.
We either touch or do not touch.

Yet the great humilities
Keep us always ill at ease.
The weather moves above us and
The mouse makes its little sound.
Whatever happens happens and
The false hands are moving round.

Hell with this and hell with that.
All that's best is better not.
Yet the great humilities
Keep us always ill at ease,
And in keeping us they go
Through the quick and through the slow.

APPROACHES TO HOW THEY BEHAVE

1

What does it matter if the words
I choose, in the order I choose them in,
Go out into a silence I know
Nothing about, there to be let
In and entertained and charmed
Out of their master's orders? And yet
I would like to see where they go
And how without me they behave.

2

Speaking is difficult and one tries
To be exact and yet not to
Exact the prime intention to death.
On the other hand the appearance of things
Must not be made to mean another
Thing. It is a kind of triumph
To see them and to put them down
As what they are. The inadequacy
Of the living, animal language drives
Us all to metaphor and an attempt
To organize the spaces we think
We have made occur between the words.

3

The bad word and the bad word and
The word which glamours me with some
Quick face it pulls to make me let
It leave me to go across
In roughly your direction, hates
To go out maybe so completely
On another silence not its own.

4

Before I know it they are out
Afloat in the head which freezes them.
Then I suppose I take the best
Away and leave the others arranged
Like floating bergs to sink a convoy.

5

One word says to its mate O
I do not think we go together
Are we doing any good here
Why do we find ourselves put down?
The mate pleased to be spoken to
Looks up from the line below
And says well that doubtful god
Who has us here is far from sure
How we on our own tickle the chin
Of the prince or the dame that lets us in.

6

The dark companion is a star
Very present like a dark poem
Far and unreadable just out
At the edge of this poem floating.
It is not more or less a dark
Companion poem to the poem.

7

Language is expensive if
We want to strut, busked out
Showing our best on silence.
Good Morning. That is a bonny doing
Of verbs you wear with the celandine
Catching the same sun as mine.
You wear your dress like a prince but
A country's prince beyond my ken.
Through the chinks in your lyric coat
My ear catches a royal glimpse
Of fuzzed flesh, unworded body.
Was there something you wanted to say?
I myself dress up in what I can
Afford on the broadway. Underneath
My overcoat of the time's slang
I am fashionable enough wearing
The grave-clothes of my generous masters.

8

And what are you supposed to say
I asked a new word but it kept mum.
I had secretly admired always
What I thought it was here for.
But I was wrong when I looked it up
Between the painted boards. It said
Something it was never very likely
I could fit in to a poem in my life.

9

The good word said I am not pressed
For time. I have all the foxglove day
And all my user's days to give
You my attention. Shines the red
Fox in the digitalis grove.
Choose me choose me. Guess which
Word I am here calling myself
The best. If you can't fit me in
To lying down here among the fox
Glove towers of the moment, say
I am yours the more you use me. Tomorrow
Same place same time give me a ring.

10

Backwards the poem's just as good.
We human angels as we read
Read back as we gobble the words up.
Allowing the poem to represent
A recognizable landscape
Sprouting green up or letting green
With all its weight of love hang
To gravity's sweet affection,
Arse-versa it is the same object,
Even although the last word seems
To have sung first, or the breakfast lark
Sings up from the bottom of the sea.

11

The poem is not a string of knots
Tied for a meaning of another time
And country, unreadable, found
By chance. The poem is not a henge
Or Easter Island emerged Longnose
Or a tally used by early unknown
Peoples. The words we breathe and puff
Are our utensils down the dream
Into the manhole. Replace the cover.

12

The words are mine. The thoughts are all
Yours as they occur behind
The bat of your vast unseen eyes.
These words are as you see them put
Down on the dead-still page. They have
No ability above their station.
Their station on silence is exact.
What you do with them is nobody's business.

13

Running across the language lightly
This morning in the hangingover
Whistling light from the window, I
Was tripped and caught into the whole
Formal scheme which Art is.
I had only meant to enjoy
Dallying between the imaginary
And imaginary's opposite
With a thought or two up my sleeve.

14

Is the word? Yes Yes. But I hear
A sound without words from another
Person I can't see at my elbow.
A sigh to be proud of. You? Me?

15

Having to construct the silence first
To speak out on I realize
The silence even itself floats
At my ear-side with a character
I have not met before. Hello
Hello I shout but that silence
Floats steady, will not be marked
By an off-hand shout. For some reason
It refuses to be broken now
By what I thought was worth saying.
If I wait a while, if I look out
At the heavy greedy rooks on the wall
It will disperse. Now I construct
A new silence I hope to break.

THE FIFTEEN DEVICES

When who we think we are is suddenly
Flying apart, splintered into
Acts we hardly recognize
As once our kin's curious children,
I find myself turning my head
Round to observe and strangely
Accept expected astonishments
Of myself manifest and yet
Bereft somehow as I float
Out in an old-fashioned slow
Motion in all directions. I hope
A value is there lurking somewhere.

Whether it is the words we try
To hold on to or some other
Suggestion of outsideness at least
Not ourselves, it is a naked
State extremely uncomfortable.

My fifteen devices of shadow and brightness
Are settling in and the Madron
Morning accepts them in their places.
Early early the real as any
Badger in the black wood
Of Madron is somewhere going
His last round, a creature of words
Waiting to be asked to help me
In my impure, too-human purpose.

With me take you. Where shall you find us?
Somewhere here between the prised
Open spaces between the flying
Apart words. For then it was
All the blown, black wobblers
Came over on the first wind
To let me see themselves looking
In from a better high flocking
Organization than mine. They make
Between them a flag flying standing
For their own country. Down the Fore
Street run the young to the school bell.

Shall I pull myself together into
Another place? I can't follow
The little young clusters of thoughts
Running down the summer side.

My fifteen devices in my work
Shop of shadow and brightness have
Their places as they stand ready
To go out to say Hello.

CLUSTERS TRAVELLING OUT

Clearly I tap to you clearly
Along the plumbing of the world
I do not know enough, not
Knowing where it ends. I tap
And tap to interrupt silence into
Manmade durations making for this
Moment a dialect for our purpose.
TAPTAP. Are you reading that taptap
I send out to you along
My element? O watch. Here they come
Opening and shutting Communication's
Gates as they approach, History's
Princes with canisters of gas
Crystals to tip and snuff me out
Strangled and knotted with my kind
Under the terrible benevolent roof.

Clearly they try to frighten me
To almost death. I am presuming
You know who I am. To answer please
Tap tap quickly along the nearest
Metal. When you hear from me
Again I will not know you. Whoever
Speaks to you will not be me.
I wonder what I will say.

Remember I am here O not else
Where in this quick disguise, this very
Thought that's yours for a moment. I sit
Here behind this tempered mesh.

I think I hear you hearing me.
I think I see you seeing me.
I suppose I am really only about
Two feet away. You must excuse
Me, have I spoken to you before?
I seem to know your face from some
One else I was, that particular
Shadow head on the other side
Of the wire in the VISITORS ROOM

I am learning to speak here in a way
Which may be useful afterwards.
Slops in hand we shuffle together,
Something to look forward to
Behind the spyhole. Here in our concrete
Soundbox we slide the jargon across
The watching air, a lipless language
Necessarily squashed from the side
To make its point against the rules.
It is our poetry such as it is.

Are you receiving those clusters
I send out travelling? Alas
I have no way of knowing or
If I am overheard here.
Is that (It is.) not what I want?

The slaughterhouse is next door.
Destroy this. They are very strict.

3

Can you see my As and Ys semaphore
Against the afterglow on the slaughterhouse
Roof where I stand on the black ridge
Waving my flagging arms to speak?

4

Corridors have their character. I know well
The ring of government boots on our concrete.
Malcolm's gone now. There's nobody to shout to.
But when they're not about in the morning I shout
HOY HOY HOY and the whole corridor rings
And I listen while my last HOY turns the elbow
With a fading surprised difference of tone and loses
Heart and in dwindling echoes vanishes away.
Each person who comes, their purpose precedes them
In how they walk. You learn to read that.
Sometimes the step's accompanied by metal
Jingling and metrical, filled with invention.
Metal opened and slammed is frightening. I try
To not be the first to speak. There is nothing to say.
Burn this. I do not dislike this place. I like
Being here. They are very kind. It's doing me good.

5

If this place I write from is real then
I must be allegorical. Or maybe
The place and myself are both the one
Side of the allegory and the other
Side is apart and still escaped
Outside. And where do you come in
With your musical key-ring and brilliant
Whistle pitched for the whipped dog?

And stands loving to recover me,
Lobe-skewers clipped to his swelling breast,
His humane-killer draped with a badged
Towel white as snow. And listen,
Ventriloquized for love his words
Gainsay any deep anguish left
For the human animal. O dear night
Cover up my beastly head.

6

Take note of who stands at my elbow listening
To all I say but not to all you hear.
She comes on Wednesdays, just on Wednesdays,
And today I make a Wednesday. On and off
I decide to make her my half-cousin Brigit
Back from the wrack and shingle on the Long Loch.
You yourself need pretend nothing. She
Is only here as an agent. She could not
On her own carry a message to you either
Written or dreamed by word of her perfect mouth.

Look. Because my words are stern and frown
She is somewhere wounded. She goes away. You see
It hasn't been a good Wednesday for her. For you
Has it been a good Wednesday? Or is yours Tuesday?

7

When the birds blow like burnt paper
Over the poorhouse roof and the slaughter
House and all the houses of Madron,
I would like to be out of myself and
About the extra, ordinary world
No matter what disguise it wears
For my sake, in my love.

It would be better than beside the Dnieper,
The Brahmaputra or a green daughter
Tributary of the Amazon.

But first I must empty my shit-bucket
And hope my case (if it can be found)
Will come up soon. I thought I heard
My name whispered on the vine.

Surrounded by howls the double-shifting
Slaughterhouse walls me in. High
On the wall I have my blue square
Through which I see the London-Cairo
Route floating like distant feathers.

I hear their freezing whistles. Reply
Carefully. They are cracking down.
Don't hurry away, I am waiting for
A message to come in now.

SLAUGHTERHOUSE

Hung on the hooks the voices scream

Nightwatching here I go my rounds
Among those voices as they hang
And drip blood in the sweet drains.
I landed this job by stealth,
For free meat and the sake of my health.

Bang at the door or I'll not hear,
With calves at the back waiting their turn.
Whoever you are, it's worth a visit.
The watchman's clock is no great company
And I'll take you round for a small fee.

I've always wanted to live in a slaughter
House of my own and take my tea
Between my rounds with the clock in harness
Hung on the wall beside the stove.
The slaughter-house is a house of Love.

THE CONSCRIPT GOES

1

Having fallen not knowing,
By what force put down or for
What reason, the young fellow raises
His dreaming bloody head. The fox
Glove towers and the whiskered rye
He sees between just. He sees
His mother wading through the field
In a uniform of the other side.
Urine and blood speak through
The warmth of his comfortable pain.

His fingers open towards her but
He is alone, only a high
International lark sings
'Hark Hark my boy among the rye.'

2

Far at home, the home he always
Was impatient of, his mother
Is making jam in a copper pan.
His mongrel he knows well lies down
To whine and knock his tail on once
The card-table's leg. Upstairs
His young sister Jean takes
A long time to get ready
To meet her boy she isn't sure
She loves or even likes or whether
To let him do everything today.

3

It is my mother wading through
The broken rye and I can see
Her plain, entering my good eye.

The approaching mother bush shocks
His fading guilt. The pain has gone.
As his parochial head nestles
Into the springing field he quite
Accurately sees a high sky-trail
Dispersing slowly to the west.

4

Father and Mother I am not here.
They stir me with a wooden spoon.
I fell. I seemed to fall. I thought
You wanted to speak to me and I turned
For a second away from what I was doing.
I am frightened of flies. Surely
You must maybe want to speak to me.

Do you think I have done something bad?
Who is right and who is wrong?
The stalks of rye rustle and
A terrible fly is on my cheek.
You know you know I am calling you.
I'll wink my good eye once for yes
And twice for no, although the lid
Is weighing a ton and not even
My pinky moves when I want it to.

5

Lark, my high bright whistler
And friend, are you still exploring
Your blue place where you see me from?
Where I am lying is any where
Near you all. Pencil and slate
Has a funny smell I can smell now
In Kelvin's School just up the road.
The girl who sat in front of me,
Her name was Janet. She liked me.

6

Dad O Mum, I know I'm cheeky.
I will be a better boy. I'll try
Better this time. You'll see you'll see.
My new suit out of Pointers?
Is it ready safe, hanging there?
Mother I didn't like it I mean
I'll be glad to get back away.
Mum, will you put me into the kitchen
To see your bright mantel-brasses
And keep the dog from licking my neck
And keep the flies off my face.
Mother, I am not well.

IMAGINE A FOREST

Imagine a forest
A real forest.

You are walking in it and it sighs
Round you where you go in a deep
Ballad on the border of a time
You have seemed to walk in before.
It is nightfall and you go through
Trying to find between the twittering
Shades the early starlight edge
Of the open moor land you know.
I have set you here and it is not a dream
I put you through. Go on between
The elephant bark of those beeches
Into that lightening, almost glade.

And he has taken
My word and gone

Through his own Ettrick darkening
Upon himself and he's come across
A glinted knight lying dying
On needles under a high tree.
Ease his visor open gently
To reveal whatever white, encased
Face will ask out at you who
It is you are or if you will
Finish him off. His eyes are open.
Imagine he does not speak. Only
His beard moving against the metal
Signs that he would like to speak.

Imagine a room
Where you are home

Taking your boots off from the wood
In that deep ballad very not
A dream and the fire noisily
Kindling up and breaking its sticks.
Do not imagine I put you there
For nothing. I put you through it
There in that holt of words between
The bearded liveoaks and the beeches
For you to meet a man alone
Slipping out of whatever cause
He thought he lay there dying for.

Hang up the ballad
Behind the door.

You are come home but you are about
To not fight hard enough and die
In a no less desolate dark wood
Where a stranger shall never enter.

Imagine a forest
A real forest.

A NOTE TO THE DIFFICULT ONE

This morning I am ready if you are,
To hear you speaking in your new language.
I think I am beginning to have nearly
A way of writing down what it is I think
You say. You enunciate very clearly
Terrible words always just beyond me.

I stand in my vocabulary looking out
Through my window of fine water ready
To translate natural occurrences
Into something beyond any idea
Of pleasure. The wisps of April fly
With light messages to the lonely.

This morning I am ready if you are
To speak. The early quick rains
Of Spring are drenching the window-glass.
Here in my words looking out
I see your face speaking flying
In a cloud wanting to say something.

THE NIGHT CITY

Unmet at Euston in a dream
Of London under Turner's steam
Misting the iron gantries, I
Found myself running away
From Scotland into the golden city.

I ran down Gray's Inn Road and ran
Till I was under a black bridge.
This was me at nineteen
Late at night arriving between
The buildings of the City of London.

And then I (O I have fallen down)
Fell in my dream beside the Bank
Of England's wall to bed, me
With my money belt of Northern ice.
I found Eliot and he said yes

And sprang into a Holmes cab.
Boswell passed me in the fog
Going to visit Whistler who
Was with John Donne who had just seen
Paul Potts shouting on Soho Green.

Midnight. I hear the moon
Light chiming on St Paul's.

The City is empty. Night
Watchmen are drinking their tea.

The Fire had burnt out.
The Plague's pits had closed
And gone into literature.

Between the big buildings
I sat like a flea crouched
In the stopped works of a watch.

ENTER A CLOUD

Gently disintegrate me
Said nothing at all.

Is there still time to say
Said I myself lying
In a bower of bramble
Into which I have fallen.

Look through my eyes up
At blue with not anything
We could have ever arranged
Slowly taking place.

Above the spires of the fox
Gloves and above the bracken
Tops with their young heads
Recognizing the wind,
The armies of the empty
Blue press me further
Into Zennor Hill.

If I half-close my eyes
The spiked light leaps in
And I am here as near
Happy as I will get
In the sailing afternoon.

Enter a cloud. Between
The head of Zennor and
Gurnard's Head the long
Marine horizon makes
A blue wall or is it
A distant table-top
Of the far-off simple sea.

Enter a cloud. O cloud,
I see you entering from
Your west gathering yourself
Together into a white
Headlong. And now you move
And stream out of the Gurnard,
The west corner of my eye.

Enter a cloud. The cloud's
Changing shape is crossing
Slowly only an inch
Above the line of the sea.
Now nearly equidistant
Between Zennor and Gurnard's
Head, an elongated
White anvil is sailing
Not wanting to be a symbol.

3

Said nothing at all.

And proceeds with no idea
Of destination along
The sea bearing changing

Messages. Jean in London,
Lifting a cup, looking
Abstractedly out through
Her Hampstead glass will never
Be caught by your new shape
Above the chimneys. Jean,
Jean, do you not see
This cloud has been thought of
And written on Zennor Hill.

4

The cloud is going beyond
What I can see or make.
Over up-country maybe
Albert Strick stops and waves
Caught in the middle of teeling
Broccoli for the winter.
The cloud is not there yet.

From Gurnard's Head To Zennor
Head the level line
Crosses my eyes lying
On buzzing Zennor Hill.

The cloud is only a wisp
And gone behind the Head.

It is funny I got the sea's
Horizontal slightly surrealist.
Now when I raise myself
Out of the bracken I see
The long empty blue
Between the fishing Gurnard
And Zennor. It was a cloud

The language at my time's
Disposal made use of.

5

Thank you. And for your applause.
It has been a pleasure. I
Have never enjoyed speaking more.
May I also thank the real ones
Who have made this possible.
First, the cloud itself. And now
Gurnard's Head and Zennor
Head. Also recognize
How I have been helped
By Jean and Madron's Albert
Strick (He is a real man.)
And good words like brambles,
Bower, spiked, fox, anvil, teeling.

The bees you heard are from
A hive owned by my friend
Garfield down there below
In the house by Zennor Church.

The good blue sun is pressing
Me into Zennor Hill.

Gently disintegrate me
Said nothing at all.

LOCH THOM

I

Just for the sake of recovering
I walked backward from fifty-six
Quick years of age wanting to see,
And managed not to trip or stumble
To find Loch Thom and turned round
To see the stretch of my childhood
Before me. Here is the loch. The same
Long-beaked cry curls across
The heather-edges of the water held
Between the hills a boyhood's walk
Up from Greenock. It is the morning.

And I am here with my mammy's
Bramble jam scones in my pocket.
The Firth is miles and I have come
Back to find Loch Thom maybe
In this light does not recognize me.

This is a lonely freshwater loch.
No farms on the edge. Only
Heather grouse-moor stretching
Down to Greenock and One Hope
Street or stretching away across
Into the blue moors of Ayrshire.

2

And almost I am back again
Wading the heather down to the edge
To sit. The minnows go by in shoals
Like iron-filings in the shallows.
My mother is dead. My father is dead
And all the trout I used to know
Leaping from their sad rings are dead.

3

I drop my crumbs into the shallow
Weed for the minnows and pinheads.
You see that I will have to rise
And turn round and get back where
My running age will slow for a moment
To let me on. It is a colder
Stretch of water than I remember.

The curlew's cry travelling still
Kills me fairly. In front of me
The grouse flurry and settle. GOBACK
GOBACK GOBACK FAREWELL LOCH THOM.

TO ALEXANDER GRAHAM

Lying asleep walking
Last night I met my father
Who seemed pleased to see me.
He wanted to speak. I saw
His mouth saying something
But the dream had no sound.

We were surrounded by
Laid-up paddle steamers
In The Old Quay in Greenock.
I smelt the tar and the ropes.

It seemed that I was standing
Beside the big iron cannon
The tugs used to tie up to
When I was a boy. I turned
To see Dad standing just
Across the causeway under
That one lamp they keep on.

He recognized me immediately.
I could see that. He was
The handsome, same age
With his good brows as when
He would take me on Sundays
Saying we'll go for a walk.

Dad, what am I doing here?
What is it I am doing now?
Are you proud of me?
Going away, I knew
You wanted to tell me something.

You stopped and almost turned back
To say something. My father,
I try to be the best
In you you give me always.

Lying asleep turning
Round in the quay-lit dark
It was my father standing
As real as life. I smelt
The quay's tar and the ropes.

I think he wanted to speak.
But the dream had no sound.
I think I must have loved him.

JOHANN JOACHIM QUANTZ'S FIVE LESSONS

THE FIRST LESSON

So that each person may quickly find that
Which particularly concerns him, certain metaphors
Convenient to us within the compass of this
Lesson are to be allowed. It is best I sit
Here where I am to speak on the other side
Of language. You, of course, in your own time
And incident (I speak in the small hours.)
Will listen from your side. I am very pleased
We have sought us out. No doubt you have read
My Flute Book. Come. The Guild clock's iron men
Are striking out their few deserted hours
And here from my high window Brueghel's winter
Locks the canal below. I blow my fingers.

THE SECOND LESSON

Good morning, Karl. Sit down. I have been thinking
About your progress and my progress as one
Who teaches you, a young man with talent
And the rarer gift of application. I think
You must now be becoming a musician
Of a certain calibre. It is right maybe
That in our lessons now I should expect
Slight and very polite impatiences
To show in you. Karl, I think it is true,
You are now nearly able to play the flute.

Now we must try higher, aware of the terrible
Shapes of silence sitting outside your ear
Anxious to define you and really love you.
Remember silence is curious about its opposite
Element which you shall learn to represent.

Enough of that. Now stand in the correct position
So that the wood of the floor will come up through you.
Stand, but not too stiff. Keep your elbows down.
Now take a simple breath and make me a shape
Of clear unchained started and finished tones.
Karl, as well as you are able, stop
Your fingers into the breathing apertures
And speak and make the cylinder delight us.

THE THIRD LESSON

Karl, you are late. The traverse flute is not
A study to take lightly. I am cold waiting.
Put one piece of coal in the stove. This lesson
Shall not be prolonged. Right. Stand in your place.

Ready? Blow me a little ladder of sound
From a good stance so that you feel the heavy
Press of the floor coming up through you and
Keeping your pitch and tone in character.

Now that is something, Karl. You are getting on.
Unswell your head. One more piece of coal.
Go on now but remember it must be always
Easy and flowing. Light and shadow must
Be varied but be varied in your mind
Before you hear the eventual return sound.

Play me the dance you made for the barge-master.
Stop stop Karl. Play it as you first thought
Of it in the hot boat-kitchen. That is a pleasure
For me. I can see I am making you good.
Keep the stove red. Hand me the matches. Now
We can see better. Give me a shot at the pipe.
Karl, I can still put on a good flute-mouth
And show you in this high cold room something
You will be famous to have said you heard.

THE FOURTH LESSON

You are early this morning. What we have to do
Today is think of you as a little creator
After the big creator. And it can be argued
You are as necessary, even a composer
Composing in the flesh an attitude
To slay the ears of the gentry. Karl,
I know you find great joy in the great
Composers. But now you can put your lips to
The messages and blow them into sound
And enter and be there as well. You must
Be faithful to who you are speaking from
And yet it is all right. You will be there.

Take your coat off. Sit down. A glass of Bols
Will help us both. I think you are good enough
To not need me anymore. I think you know
You are not only an interpreter.

What you will do is always something else
And they will hear you simultaneously with
The Art you have been given to read. Karl,

I think the Spring is really coming at last.
I see the canal boys working. I realize
I have not asked you to play the flute today.
Come and look. Are the barges not moving?
You must forgive me. I am not myself today.
Be here on Thursday. When you come, bring
Me five herrings. Watch your fingers. Spring
Is apparent but it is still chilblain weather.

THE LAST LESSON

Dear Karl, this morning is our last lesson.
I have been given the opportunity to
Live in a certain person's house and tutor
Him and his daughters on the traverse flute.
Karl, you will be all right. In those recent
Lessons my heart lifted to your playing.

I know. I see you doing well, invited
In a great chamber in front of the gentry. I
Can see them with their dresses settling in
And bored mouths beneath moustaches sizing
You up as you are, a lout from the canal
With big ears but an angel's tread on the flute.

But you will be all right. Stand in your place
Before them. Remember Johann. Begin with good
Nerve and decision. Do not intrude too much
Into the message you carry and put out.

One last thing, Karl, remember when you enter
The joy of those quick high archipelagoes,
To make to keep your finger-stops as light
As feathers but definite. What can I say more?
Do not be sentimental or in your Art.
I will miss you. Do not expect applause.

LINES ON ROGER HILTON'S WATCH

Which I was given because
I loved him and we had
Terrible times together.

O tarnished ticking time
Piece with your bent hand,
You must be used to being
Looked at suddenly
In the middle of the night
When he switched the light on
Beside his bed. I hope
You told him the best time
When he lifted you up
To meet the Hilton gaze.

I lift you up from the mantel
Piece here in my house
Wearing your verdigris.
At least I keep you wound
And put my ear to you
To hear Botallack tick.

You realize your master
Has relinquished you
And gone to lie under
The ground at St Just.

Tell me the time. The time
Is Botallack o'clock.
This is the dead of night.

He switches the light on
To find a cigarette
And pours himself a Teachers.
He picks me up and holds me
Near his lonely face
To see my hands. He thinks
He is not being watched.

The images of his dream
Are still about his face
As he spits and tries not
To remember where he was.

I am only a watch
And pray time hastes away.
I think I am running down.

Watch, it is time I wound
You up again. I am
Very much not your dear
Last master but we had
Terrible times together.

THE FOUND PICTURE

1

Flame and the garden we are together
In it using our secret time up.
We are together in this picture.

It is of the Early Italian School
And not great, a landscape
Maybe illustrating a fable.

We are those two figures barely
Discernible in the pool under
The umbra of the foreground tree.

Or that is how I see it. Nothing
Will move. This is a holy picture
Under its varnish darkening.

2

The Tree of Life unwraps its leaves
And makes its fruit like lightning.
Beyond the river the olive groves.

Beyond the olives musical sounds
Are heard. It is the old, authentic
Angels weeping out of bounds.

3

Observe how the two creatures turn
Slowly toward each other each
In the bare buff and yearning in

Their wordless place. The light years
Have over-varnished them to keep
Them still in their classic secrets.

I slant the canvas. Now look in
To where under the cracking black,
A third creature hides by the spring.

The painted face is faded with light
And the couple are aware of him.
They turn their tufts out of his sight

In this picture's language not
Wanting to be discovered. He
Is not a bad man or a caught

Tom peeping out of his true time.
He is a god making a funny
Face across the world's garden.

See they are fixed they cannot move
Within the landscape of our eyes.
What shall we say out of love

Turning toward each other to hide
In somewhere the breaking garden?
What shall we say to the hiding god?

DEAR BRYAN WYNTER

I

This is only a note
To say how sorry I am
You died. You will realize
What a position it puts
Me in. I couldn't really
Have died for you if so
I were inclined. The carn
Foxglove here on the wall
Outside your first house
Leans with me standing
In the Zennor wind.

Anyhow how are things?
Are you still somewhere
With your long legs
And twitching smile under
Your blue hat walking
Across a place? Or am
I greedy to make you up
Again out of memory?
Are you there at all?
I would like to think
You were all right
And not worried about
Monica and the children
And not unhappy or bored.

2

Speaking to you and not
Knowing if you are there
Is not too difficult.
My words are used to that.
Do you want anything?
Where shall I send something?
Rice-wine, meanders, paintings
By your contemporaries?
Or shall I send a kind
Of news of no time
Leaning against the wall
Outside your old house.

The house and the whole moor
Is flying in the mist.

3

I am up. I've washed
The front of my face
And here I stand looking
Out over the top
Half of my bedroom window.
There almost as far
As I can see I see
St Buryan's church tower.
An inch to the left, behind
That dark rise of woods,
Is where you used to lurk.

4

This is only a note
To say I am aware
You are not here. I find
It difficult to go
Beside Housman's star
Lit fences without you.
And nobody will laugh
At my jokes like you.

5

Bryan, I would be obliged
If you would scout things out
For me. Although I am not
Just ready to start out.
I am trying to be better,
Which will make you smile
Under your blue hat.

I know I make a symbol
Of the foxglove on the wall.
It is because it knows you.

FALLING INTO THE SEA

Breathing water is easy
If you put your mind to it.
The little difficulty
Of the first breath
Is soon got over. You
Will find everything right.

Keep your eyes open
As you go fighting down
But try to keep it easy
As you meet the green
Skylight rising up
Dying to let you through.

Then you will seem to want
To stand like a sea-horse
In the new suspension.
Don't be frightened. Breathe
Deeply and you will go down
Blowing your silver worlds.

Now you go down turning
Slowly over from fathom
To fathom even remembering
Unexpected small
Corners of the dream
You have been in. Now

What has happened to you?

You have arrived on the sea
Floor and a lady comes out
From the Great Kelp Wood
And gives you some scones and a cup
Of tea and asks you
If you come here often.

THE VISIT

How would you like to be killed or are
You in disguise the one to take
Me back? I don't want to go back
As I am now. I'm not dressed
For the sudden wind out of the West.

Also sometimes I get lost.
If I stay on for a bit and try
Upside-down to speak and cry
HELP ME, HELP ME, will anything
Happen? Will I begin to sing?

What a fine get-up you have on,
Mister, if that is your entering name.
How did you get through the window-frame
To stand beside me? I am a simple
Boy from Greenock who could kill

You easily if it was not you.
Please tell me if you come on business.
You are too early. I have to kiss
My dear and another dear and the natural
Objects as well as my writing table.

Goodnight. I will mend the window.
Thank you for giving me time
To kiss the lovely living game.
So he went away
Without having touched me.

He looked at me with courage.
His head was a black orange.

I WILL LEND YOU MALCOLM

I will lend you Malcolm
    Mooney my friend to seem
To take you out to find whatever it is
You need or think you need across the ice.
Deep in the berg there is a freezing office
    With an emerald window
    Waiting to deal with you.

I will lend you my wooden
    Goggles with slits in
To save your eyes from the literature of the snow.
Take nothing not necessary. Mister Mooney
Will look after you wherever you wish to go.
    Take care of my dogs.
    But Malcolm will do that.

Give them a good crack
    An inch above the ear
And there you are holding on and travelling
Out of this poem with the dogs yelping
With joy to go somewhere or to bring
    You further out to find
    Your home in the white wind.

O WHY AM I SO BRIGHT

O why am I so bright
Flying in the night?

Why am I so fair
Flying through the air?

Will you let me in
After all I've done?

You are a good boy
On the fields of joy.

We see you as you go
Across the fields of snow.

We will not let you in.
Never. Never. Never.

TO MY WIFE AT MIDNIGHT

I

Are you to say goodnight
And turn away under
The blanket of your delight?

Are you to let me go
Alone to sleep beside you
Into the drifting snow?

Where we each reach,
Sleeping alone together,
Nobody can touch.

Is the cat's window open?
Shall I turn into your back?
And what is to happen?

What is to happen to us
And what is to happen to each
Of us asleep in our places?

I mean us both going
Into sleep at our ages
To sleep and get our fairing.

They have all gone home.
Night beasts are coming out.
The black wood of Madron

Is just waking up.
I hear the rain outside
To help me to go to sleep.

Nessie, don't let my soul
Skip and miss a beat
And cause me to fall.

3

Are you asleep I say
Into the back of your neck
For you not to hear me.

Are you asleep? I hear
Your heart under the pillow
Saying my dear my dear

My dear for all it's worth.
Where is the dun's moor
Which began your breath?

Ness, to tell you the truth
I am drifting away
Down to fish for the saithe.

Is the cat's window open?
The weather is on my shoulder
And I am drifting down

Into O can you hear me
Among your Dunsmuir Clan?
Are you coming out to play?

Did I behave badly
On the field at Culloden?
I lie sore-wounded now

By all activities, and
The terrible acts of my time
Are only a distant sound.

With responsibility
I am drifting off
Breathing regularly

Into my younger days
To play the games of Greenock
Beside the sugar-house quays.

Nessie Dunsmuir, I say
Wheesht wheesht to myself
To help me now to go

Under into somewhere
In the redcoat rain.
Buckle me for the war.

Are you to say goodnight
And kiss me and fasten
My drowsy armour tight?

My dear camp-follower,
Hap the blanket round me
And tuck in a flower.

Maybe from my sleep
In the stoure at Culloden
I'll see you here asleep

In your lonely place.